DOUBLE
BASS DRUM
INTEGRATION

FOR THE JAZZ/FUSION DRUMMER

To access audio visit:
www.halleonard.com/mylibrary

T0081344

Enter Code
7918-8978-6408-0513

HENRIQUE DE ALMEIDA

Berklee Press

Editor in Chief: Jonathan Feist
Vice President of Online Learning and Continuing Education: Debbie Cavalier
Assistant Vice President of Operations for Berklee Media: Robert F. Green
Assistant Vice President of Marketing and Recruitment for Berklee Media: Mike King
Dean of Continuing Education: Carin Nuernberg
Editorial Assistants: Matthew Dunkle, Reilly Garrett, Zoë Lustri, José Rodrigo Vazquez
Cover Design: Ranya Karifilly, Small Mammoth Design
Cover Photos: Leon Felipe Muñoz

ISBN 978-0-87639-148-8

1140 Boylston Street
Boston, MA 02215-3693 USA
(617) 747-2146

Visit Berklee Press Online at
www.berkleepress.com

Study with
■ **BERKLEE ONLINE**

online.berklee.edu

DISTRIBUTED BY

HAL•LEONARD®
CORPORATION
7777 W. BLUEMOUND RD. P.O. BOX 13819
MILWAUKEE, WISCONSIN 53213

Visit Hal Leonard Online at
www.halleonard.com

Berklee Press, a publishing activity of Berklee College of Music, is a not-for-profit educational publisher.
Available proceeds from the sales of our products are contributed to the scholarship funds of the college.

CONTENTS

AUDIO

Excerpt 1. "The Speed of Heat" by the USAF Academy Band
Excerpt 2. Open Live Solo with the USAFA Falconaires Big Band
Excerpt 3. Live Drum Solo at the Berklee Performance Center
Excerpt 4. Drum Solo with the USAFA Falconaires Big Band
Excerpt 5. Double Bass Drum Control Example
Excerpt 6. Duet with Steve Hunt
Timetable I
Timetable II
Duple-Feel Endurance Exercises
Duple-Feel Grooves
Triple-Feel Endurance Exercises
Triple-Feel Grooves
"One for Kelly"
"Hip Shuffle"
"The Dave Weckl 3"
"Shifting Time"
Triple-Feel Groove Ideas
"Weckling This"
"Weckling That"
Duple Bursts 1 and 2 with Rhythmic Interpretation
Duple Bursts 3 and 4 with Rhythmic Interpretation
"Bursting Out of Here"
Triple Bursts 1 and 2 with Rhythmic Interpretation
Triple Bursts 3 and 4 with Rhythmic Interpretation
"Bursting Out of There"
Triplet Feel Linear Exercises
"Linear Triplets"
Duple Feel Linear Exercise
"Linear Duple-Feel" Etude
False Triplet Roll, Single Hand Exerciss
"The B Line"
Single Quads
Single Quads Timetable
Quasi Quads
Double Quads Timetable
"Heavy Weather"
"Six Reasons"
"Paradoubles"

ACKNOWLEDGMENT

I would like to say thanks to my wife Erika and my two boys Max and Miles for their love, support, and endless enthusiasm and faith in me.

Thanks to my parents Dr. Gilbert Lobo De Almeida, and Conceicao De Almeida for loving me so much, and thanks to Nancy and Jary Reppen, the best in-laws in the universe!

Thanks to the Berklee College of Music Leadership, President Mr. Roger Brown, Vice President Larry Simpson, Percussion Department Chair John Ramsay, and Vice Chair Yoron Israel for providing an amazing musical environment to all of us. Thanks to Jonathan Feist, Reilly Garrett, Zoë Lustri, and Matt Dunkle at Berklee Press for being such a great team to work with.

A big thanks to my dear friend, Steve Hunt, for providing me with a great working environment during the recording of this project.

I would like to mention some of the main players who inspired me to creatively use double bass drums in a way that brings all parts of the drum set together: Louie Bellson, Billy Cobham, Narada Michael Walden, Pierre Favre, Terry Bozzio, Simon Philips, Akira Jimbo, Steve Smith, Gregg Bissonette, Dennis Chambers, Virgil Donati, Thomas Lang, Marco Minnemann, Chad Wackerman, Vinnie Colaiuta, Dave Weckl, Horacio Hernandez, Antonio Sanchez, and Carter Beauford.

They inspired me to unify the snare drum; tom toms, floor toms, percussion, and cymbals in such a way that integrates the double bass drum or pedal into the entire drum set. This concept is a bit different than the type of playing that is primarily made of incessant continuous playing that is mainly led by the feet. I found that "integrated" double bass playing involving space, dynamics, control, and a variety of rhythm structures, can be utilized in a vast majority of styles, such as jazz, rock, Brazilian, Afro-Cuban, fusion, etc. I hope that this book brings attention to alternative concepts and propositions that the double bass drum and/or double bass pedal is just a piece of equipment to be used musically, and it is not limited to the use of one particular style.

Finally, a huge thanks to Andrew Shreve and Arturo Gil at Paiste cymbals, Jennifer Vierling at Yamaha drums, Joe Testa and Neil Larrivee at Vic Firth sticks, Steve Lobmeier at Evans drumheads, Steve Negohosian at LP Percussion, and Kim Hilton at Earthworks high fidelity microphones.

I dedicate this book to all my music students at Berklee College of Music, past, present, and future. You all are an inspiration and the reason I love teaching and learning enthusiastically more and more.

INTRODUCTION

The materials in this workbook were originally created for my live private drum set lessons and other classes that I teach at Berklee College of Music, in Boston, MA. This book is intended as an organized and compact resource to be used as an introduction to certain double bass concepts for intermediate and advanced drum set students.

This book presents new, flexible principles and applications for integrating multi-pedal ideas on the drum set. It introduces many ideas that will facilitate and build an extraordinary double bass vocabulary. These ideas are not directly associated with any specific styles. Thus, their execution and musical performance applications are endless. By diligently studying these lessons, you will be able to fluently integrate multi-pedal ideas into any orchestration and in any style—particularly jazz, funk, rock, pop, Afro-Caribbean, West African, Indian, Brazilian, New Orleans, and others.

The term *rhythmic interpretation* is often used here. "Interpreting a rhythm" means changing the feel and style, embellishing the rhythms by adding notes before and/or after a figure, and also embellishing it musically by orchestrating on the drum set.

I recommend the following rhythm books as additional rich resources of basic rhythmic ideas, to be played with the exercises presented here:

- *Progressive Steps to Syncopation for the Modern Drummer* by Ted Reed
- *Modern Reading Text in 4/4* by Louie Bellson
- *Odd Time Reading Text* by Louie Bellson
- *The New Breed I* by Gary Chester

Have fun!

Henrique De Almeida

January, 2014

INTRODUCTION TO THE MUSICAL APPLICATION EXCERPTS

CD tracks 1 to 6 are musical applications of the ideas presented in this book. The concepts presented here are a collection of flexible ideas unattached to any specific styles. As you will hear, I am able to forge double bass ideas in many different musical situations:

- jazz combos
- big bands
- fusion groups
- Afro-Cuban ensembles
- Brazilian ensembles
- and even concert band!

I hope you enjoy listening to them, and that they inspire a new generation of integrated double-bass playing.

Excerpt 1

Excerpt 1. "The Speed of Heat" by the USAF Academy Band

This drum solo is extracted from a performance with the USAF Academy Concert Band. Some of the techniques and concepts used here include:

1. power fills from lesson 12
2. linear ideas from the etude "Heavy Weather" in lesson 11
3. polyrhythms, power shuffles, coordination, and the Weckl triplets from lesson 4
4. false triplets from lesson 10
5. timetable rhythms from lesson 1

Excerpt 2

Excerpt 2. Open Live Solo with the USAFA Falconaires Big Band

A home recording from the mixing board. Some of the techniques and concepts used here include:

1. polyrhythms, power fills, and coordination from lesson 4
2. ideas involving triplets and sixteenth-note double bass control exercises from lesson 1
3. ideas taken from the "Shifting Time" etude in lesson 4
4. ideas from "Weckling This" etude from lesson 5
5. rhythms from the timetable exercises in lesson 1
6. power fills from lesson 12

Excerpt 3

Excerpt 3. Live Drum Solo at the Berklee Performance Center

Some of the techniques and concepts used here include:

1. false triplets from lesson 10
2. power fills from lesson 12
3. linear triplets from lesson 9
4. double quads from lesson 11
5. single quads from lesson 11

Excerpt 4

Excerpt 4. Drum Solo with the USAFA Falconaires Big Band

This is a performance of my original composition entitle "Deixa Falar" ("Carnival" is the alternate title), originally recorded on my CD, *Samba Songs*, rearranged here by John Dawson for the USAFA Falconaires Big Band, on their CD *Sharing the Freedom*. Some of the techniques and concepts used here include:

1. power fills from lesson 12
2. false triplets from lesson 10
3. linear triplets from lesson 9
4. double quads from lesson 11

Excerpt 5

Excerpt 5. Double Bass Drum Control Example

Although this is not great quality, soundwise, the ideas here are quite interesting to me because they involve two bass drums: an 18-inch tuned with open sound, and a 20-inch bass drum tuned to be a bit more muffled. The concept to notice here is the sixteenth-note double bass control technique from lesson 1.

Excerpt 6

Excerpt 6. Duet with Steve Hunt

This one is a studio recording with my dear friend and world-class jazz fusion keyboardist and music partner, Steve Hunt. This recording is a first take, I had never played the track before and there were no charts! I love the intensity of the unknown and the urgency of improvised reaction to the track. Some of the techniques and concepts used here include:

1. sixteenth-note double-pedal control from lesson 1
2. time shifting from the "Shifting Time" etude from lesson 4
3. ideas from the "Six Reasons" etude from lesson 11
4. power fills from lesson 12
5. double quads from lesson 11

DRUM KEY

Use alternate strokes (RLRL or LRLR) on the double bass drums unless other-
wise indicated.

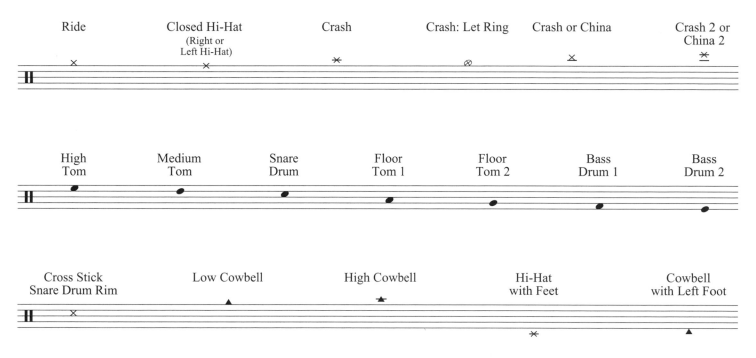

X-Hat indicates a secondary hi-hat.

Duple-Feel Constant Flow Exercises

TIMETABLE I WITH DOUBLE BASS DRUM

This timetable is a great tool to practice continuous double bass roll slow to fast and back to slow again. In other words, the first time play from measure one to measure eight, and on the repeat, begin with measure eight and play in reverse to measure one. Play at first just with the feet. Practice singles and try also with double strokes.

Timetable I

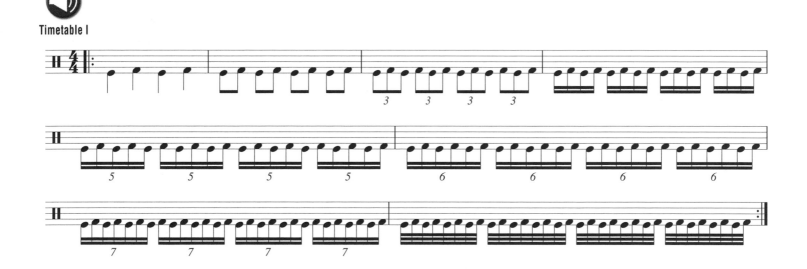

TIMETABLE II WITH HI-HAT AND SNARE DRUM

After you can play the exercise up and down without stopping, try to add the hands. At first, just try a simple rock beat with snare drum backbeats on 2 and 4, with eighth notes on closed hi-hats or a ride cymbal.

Timetable II

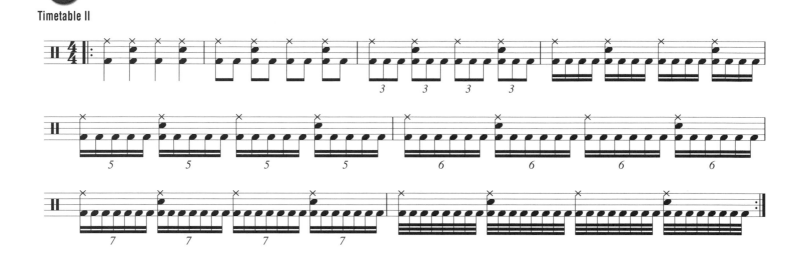

SIXTEENTH-NOTE DOUBLE-PEDAL CONTROL

These exercises are designed as a daily warm-up routine. Play as many as you can by connecting one to the next.

At first, play them just with the feet. Then, incorporate the hands, playing a simple rock groove along with the exercises. This will be a good foundation for multi-pedal setups. The exercises can be used in lateral motion, moving the different sticking from, let's say, a bass drum footboard to a hi-hat footboard to a cowbell with the foot, and so forth.

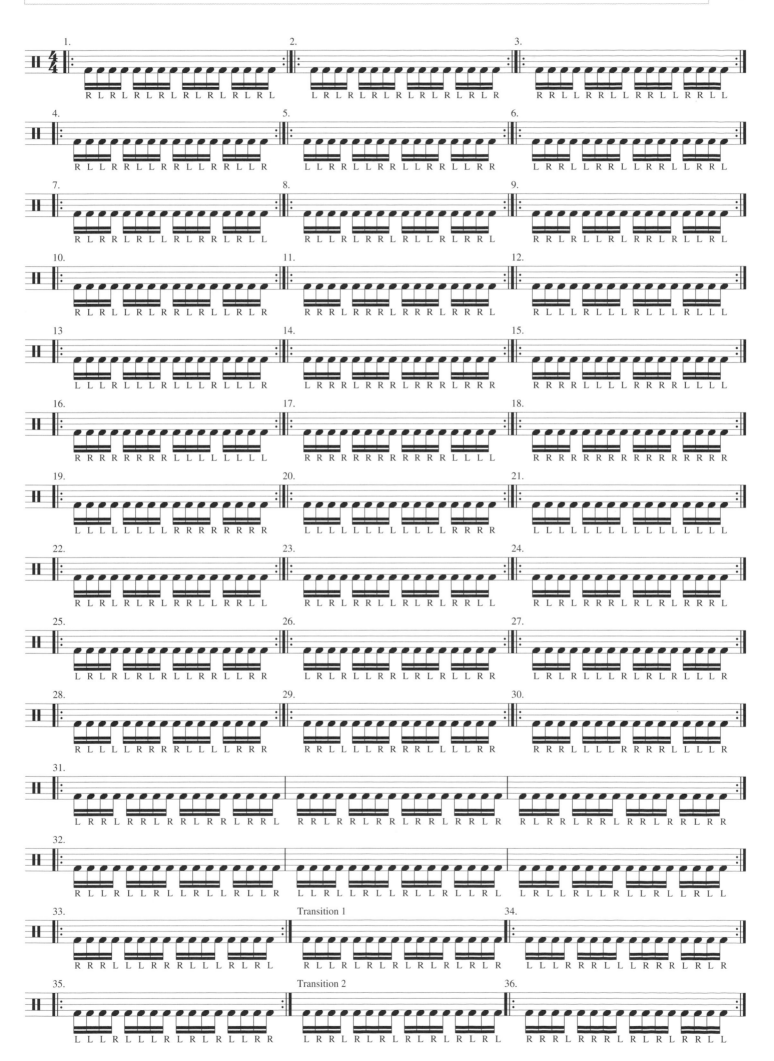

Duple-Feel Endurance Exercises

These exercises are foundational for developing endurance and speed. Practice them with the feet and snare drum only. After you are comfortable reading all the rhythms correctly, try adding the hi-hat. Note that the double-time thirty-second notes are played between each "Groove Zero" measure. This is where you rest for a moment by playing half speed, going to sixteenth notes. Then, play the next exercise going double time again. This way, you are going from sixteenth to thirty-second notes, back and forth.

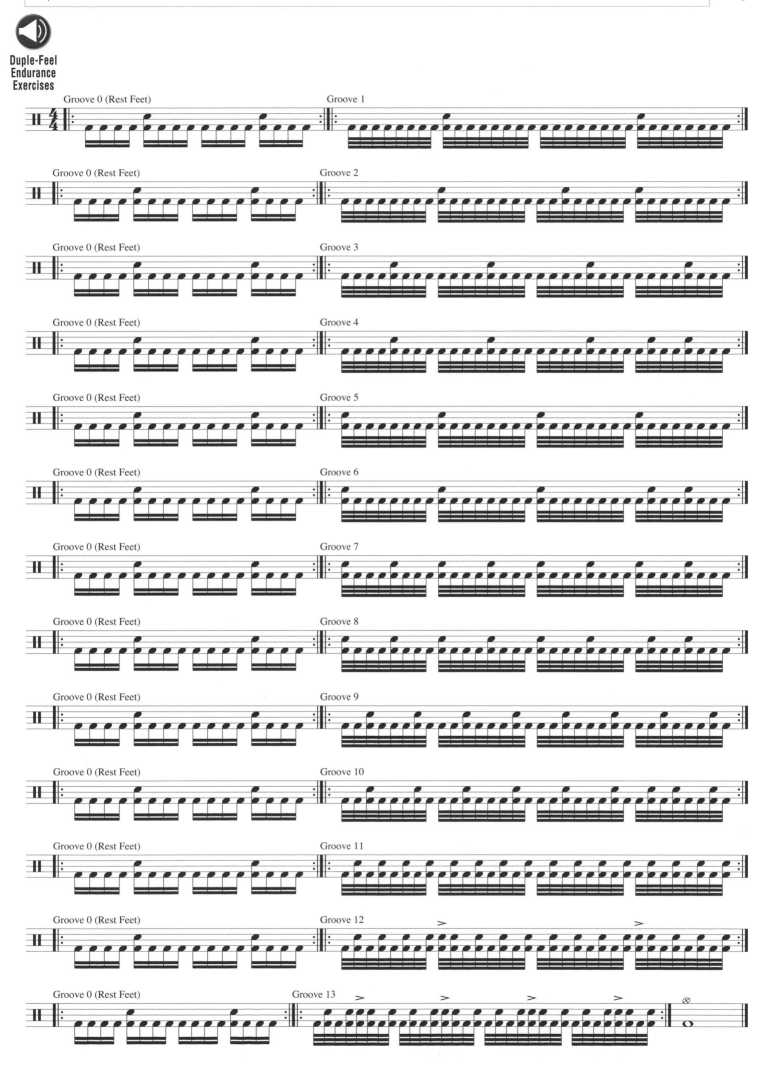

Duple-Feel Grooves

In these exercises, you will develop endurance by playing all the duple-feel grooves without a pause. You can start by playing as written, only playing twice each. As you get more comfortable, increase the amount of repetition.

Duple-Feel Grooves

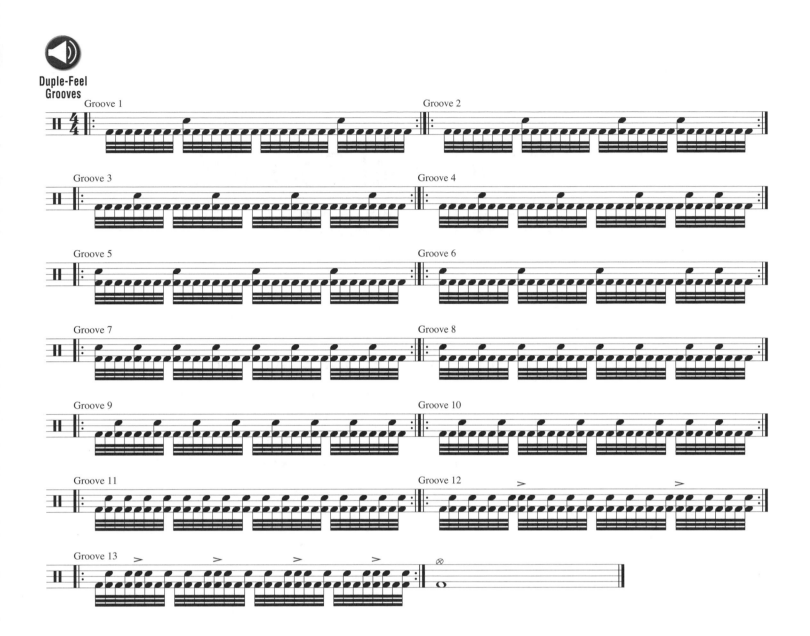

Triplet-Feel Constant Flow Exercises

EIGHTH-NOTE TRIPLET DOUBLE BASS CONTROL

These exercises are designed as a daily warm-up routine. Play as many as you can by connecting one to the next.

At first, play them just with the feet. Then, incorporate the hands, playing a simple rock shuffle groove along with the exercises. This will be a good foundation for multi-pedal setups. The exercises can be used in lateral motion, moving the different pedaling between instruments.

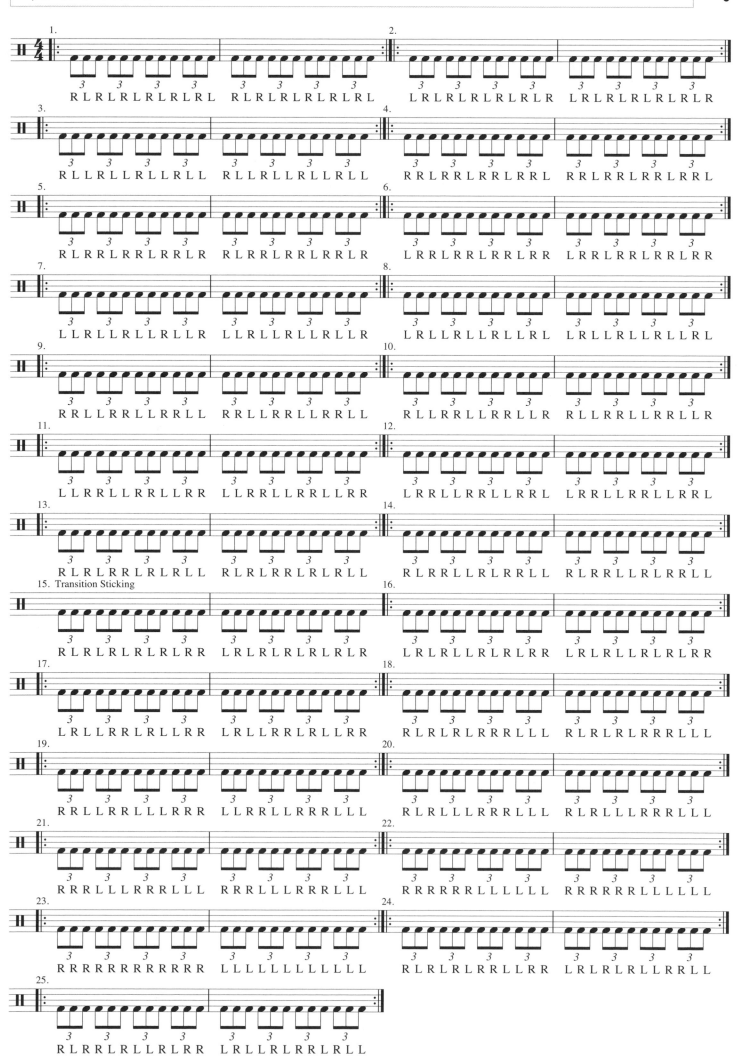

TRIPLE-FEEL ENDURANCE EXERCISES

These exercises will help you develop endurance and speed. Practice them with the feet and snare drum only. After you are comfortable reading all the rhythms correctly, try adding the hi-hat. Note that the eighth-note triplets are played between a simple shuffle groove. Rest for a moment by playing a shuffle of your choice; then, move onto the next exercise, playing constant triplets again. This way, you are going from "power shuffle" with eighth-note triplets to a simple single-pedal shuffle groove, and back and forth.

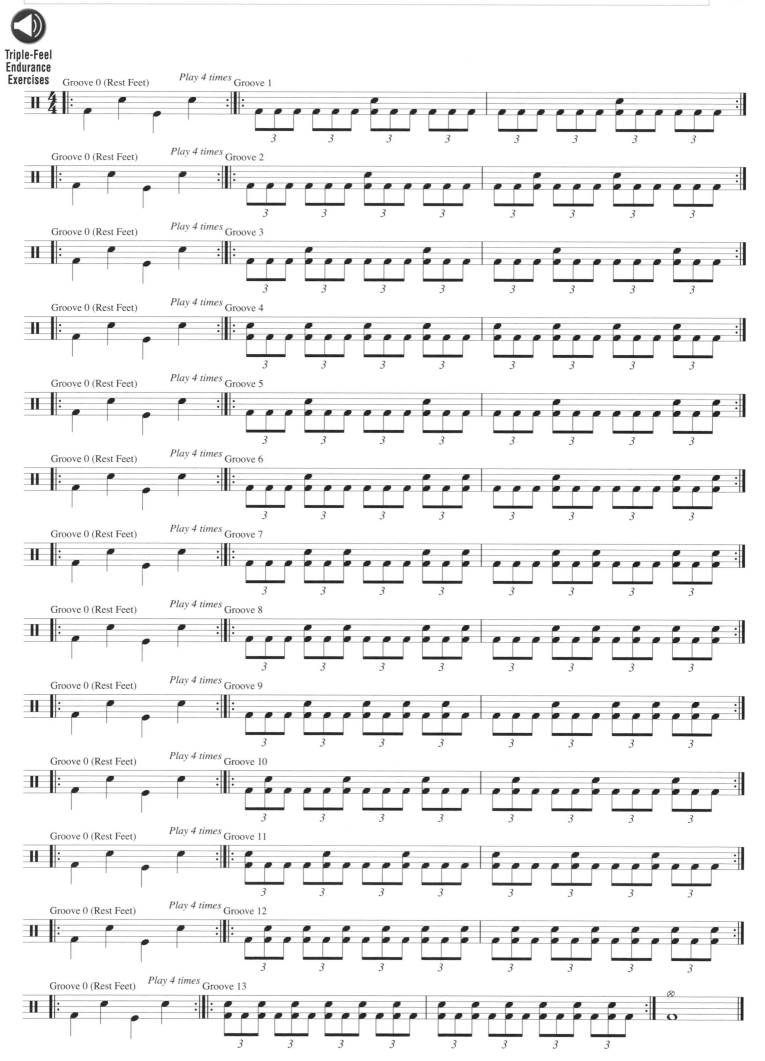

TRIPLE-FEEL GROOVES

In these exercises, you will develop endurance by playing all the power shuffle grooves without a pause. You can start by playing as written, two times each. As you get comfortable, increase the number of repetitions.

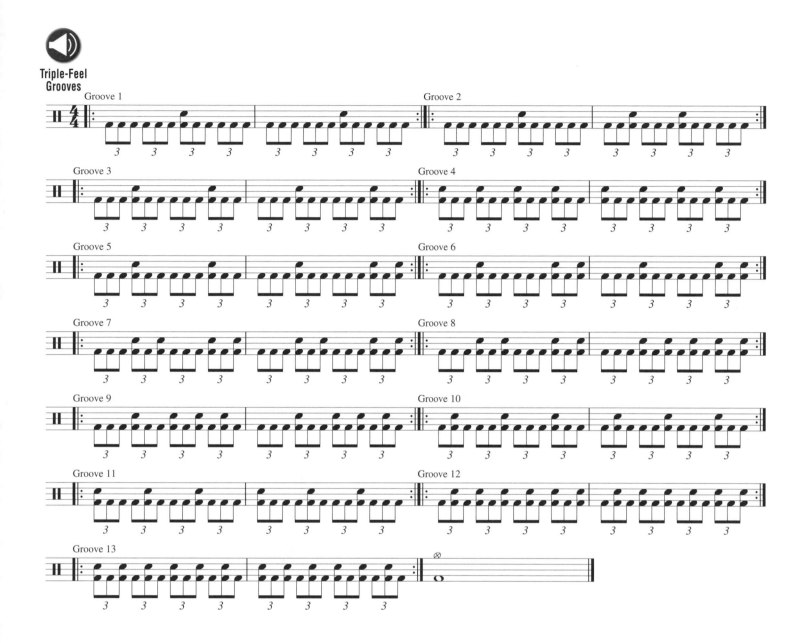

Etudes

"ONE FOR KELLY"

This etude is dedicated to a dear friend and drummer/producer, Kelly Burns from Colorado. It includes four different time feels. Section A is a relaxed eighth-note rock feel, which I play as eighth notes on a closed hi-hat accenting every first eighth note of every beat. In section B, we go into a more hip-hop feel, still eighth notes, but now emphasizing every eighth note to create an insistent eighth-note pulse.

Section C should be softer, now with sixteenth notes on the hi-hat supporting the thirty-second note bursts with the feet. (See lesson 6 for more about bursts.) Finally, in section D, we go into a power rock feel in constant sixteenth notes with the feet. Note the crash accents.

After you can play the solo comfortably, try embellishing the snare drum and cymbal parts to add your own interpretation. Remember, the most important thing is to groove, play relaxed, and make this sound good with a clear sound and well-balanced feel.

One for Kelly

Henrique De Almeida

Performance Notes:

Hi-Hat and Ride Ostinatos: Eighth and/or Sixteenth Notes

Form 1

AA BB CC

AA BB CC DD FINE

Form 2

AA BB CC DD

AA BB CC DD FINE

"HIP SHUFFLE"

This etude will help you practice leading and ending figures with the right foot and/or left foot.

Section A could be playing over quarter notes on the hi-hat or a shuffled hi-hat pattern of your choice. If you are a right-foot lead player, you will end some of the figures with the left foot. Section B adds longer figures containing five-note bursts with the feet. The end of section B is a power fusion shuffle inspired by the great Billy Cobham. Play this section (at measure 9) seven times, riding the crash or china cymbal aggressively. Section B ends with a drum fill going back to the beginning.

Section C provides plenty of opportunity to practice alternating feet on the end of several figures. In section D, we see shuffle-feel eighth notes and a six-note foot burst before returning to section D again.

The etude ends with a constant flow of triplets, with the feet in unison with the hands. The idea here is to create an opportunity for improvisation and interpretation. Try first playing measure 25 on only the snare and double bass. Then try orchestrating the triplets all over the kit, creating a dramatic ending with power fills in the last two measures.

This is a fun etude to play, with a challenging ending.

Hip Shuffle

Henrique De Almeida

LESSON 4

Polyrhythms, Power Shuffles, and Coordination Exercises

FUSION TRIPLETS: "THE DAVE WECKL 3"

The great jazz-fusion drummer Dave Weckl uses a very effective way to play constant triplets by using a LRR sticking. He also converts this three-note sticking to play in sixteenth notes. The following exercises explore some basic possibilities using the Dave Weckl 3.

Note that exercises 3, 4, and 5 are to be played six times and not eight times. Playing them six times will allow the left foot to land on beat 1.

Exercises 6, 7, and 8 can be played eight times. This creates a 4-against-3 pattern in the left foot. The left foot, however, will still resolve on every downbeat in the meter of 3/4.

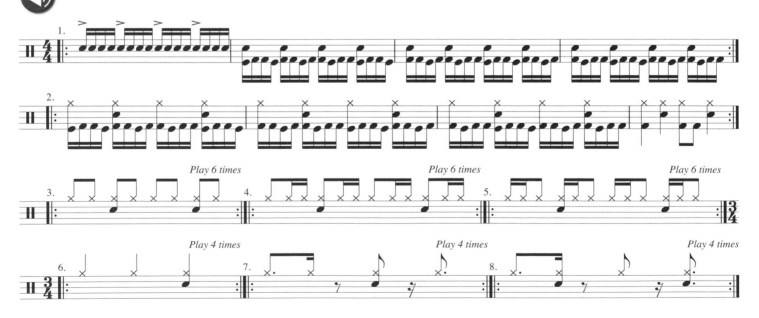

"SHIFTING TIME" ETUDE

Play a flow of sixteenth notes using the LRR pedaling with the feet. Then read the etude on the following page over the feet ostinato. This is a good opportunity to practice moving the left foot to a hi-hat and/or cowbell footboard to create polyrhythms.

Shifting Time

TRIPLE-FEEL GROOVE IDEAS

Here are some rock shuffle ideas using the Weckl 3 sticking, LRR.

COORDINATION OF DOUBLE BASS

Here, we have 3-against-4 note groupings. This is a fun way to strengthen the left hand while working with the double bass. The left hand will be playing moving accents on the snare drum while keeping a groove with the feet and a right-hand cymbal ostinato. Play each exercise three times, six times, or twelve times, with the three-bar ostinato played between each exercise. The understanding of the Moeller technique will be beneficial in executing the accents presented here. For more information on the Moeller technique, refer to Henrique De Almeida's DVD, *The Moeller Technique Workshop.*

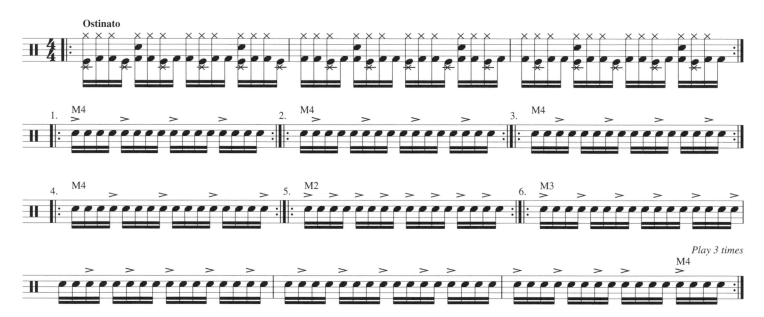

Etudes

"WECKLING THIS"

This is an interesting etude that involves a rock shuffle, a 6/8 groove, rudiments applications, power fills, and polyrhythmic concepts.

It is a straightforward power-shuffle groove throughout. Things to look out for are:

- Fourth measure of section B, the triplets are accented on every fourth note, creating 3-against-4 rhythms.

- At C, we have a paradiddle for two measures going to a 6/8 groove using double paradiddles.

- In the second part of section C, we have paradiddle sticking accented in different sound sources.

- Back to A then play AA, BB, and then take the coda. The coda is a power fill ending lasting for the last nine measures.

Weckling This

Henrique De Almeida

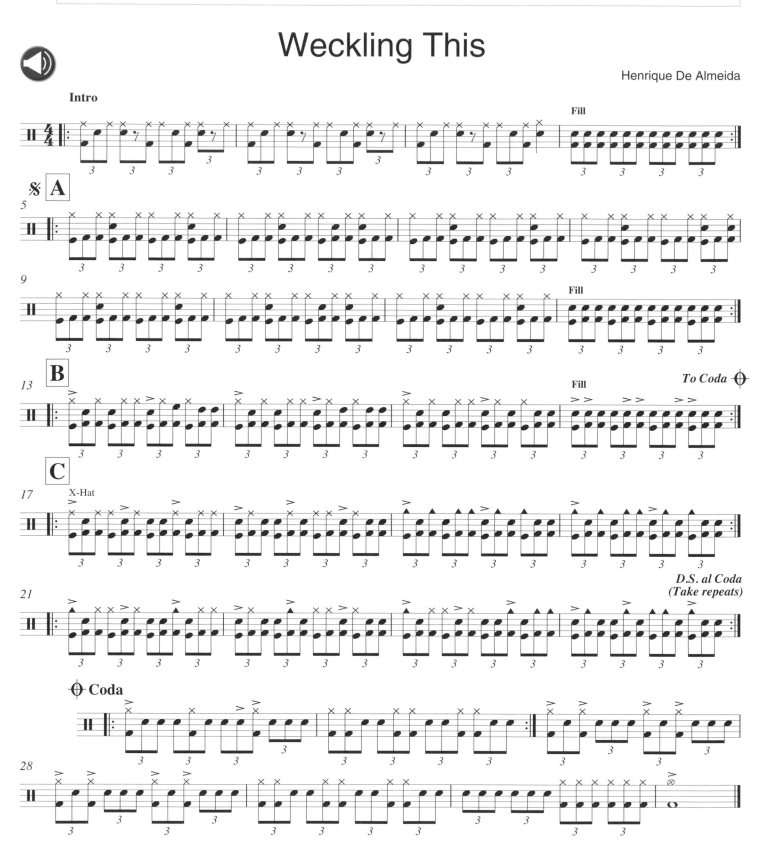

"WECKLING THAT"

The challenge in this etude is to keep the Weckl 3 throughout the piece.

In the beginning, we play a measure of sixteenth notes establishing the feel for the rhythmic base of the solo. Playing this four times creates an insistent sixteenth-note feel that will hopefully be ingrained mentally, until we go to section A. At section C, we superimpose a mambo feel going back to A. Then at D, the left hand is quite involved in creating melodic lines in the tom toms.

Weckling That

Henrique De Almeida

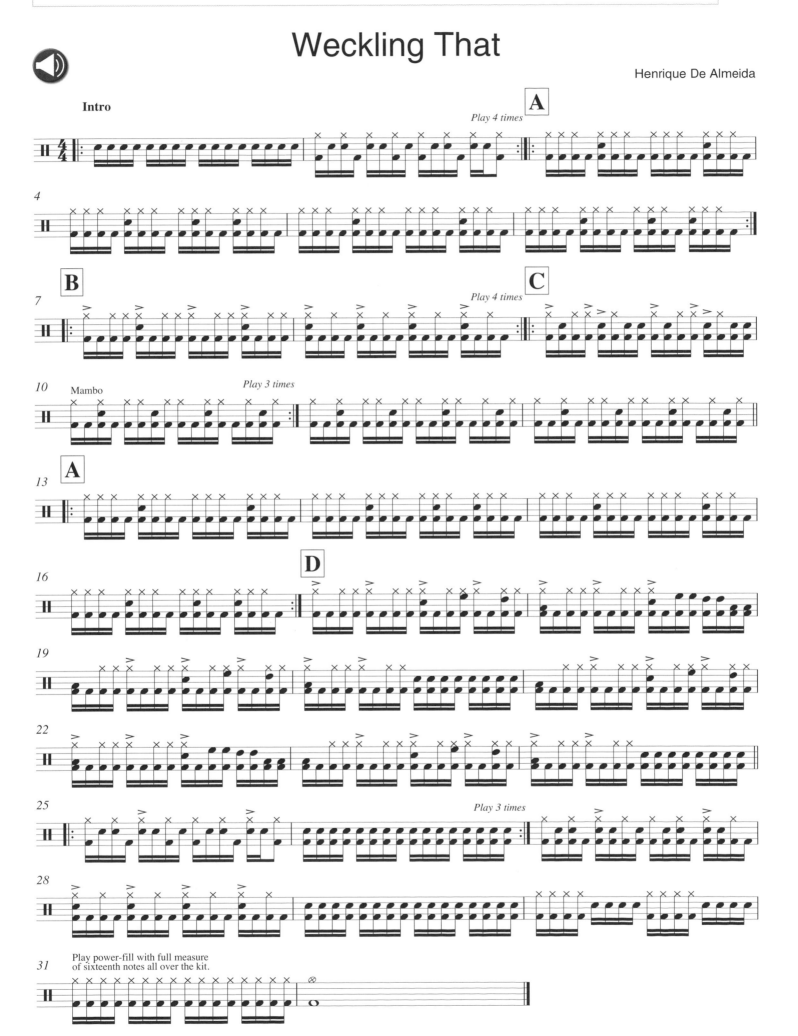

Duple-Feel Bursts and Double Bass Etude

Bursts are rapid rhythmic riffs played at speeds faster than the regular note rating of any time feel, usually played twice as fast. For example, if playing a sixteenth pop/rock/Latin groove, a burst usually will be in thirty-second notes.

TYPES OF BURST

Duple Bursts 1 & 2 with Rhythmic Interpretation (0:00–0:06)

Burst 1. Four Notes with the Feet, One Note with the Hand

Duple Bursts 1 & 2 with Rhythmic Interpretation (0:06–0:11)

Burst 2. Eight Notes with the Feet, One Note with the Hands

Rhythmic Interpretation

Since four is half of eight, we can then interpret ideas incorporating, for example, eighth notes and quarter notes by embellishing the quarter notes and the eighth notes with the bursts 1 and 2. Developing the discipline to practice those types of thing is a challenge that we can overcome by reading texts such as *Progressive Steps to Syncopation for the Modern Drummer* by Ted Reed and *Modern Reading Text in 4/4* by Louie Bellson and Gil Breines. These are great sources of rhythmic ideas.

Duple Bursts 1 & 2 with Rhythmic Interpretation (0:11–0:25)

When playing Burst 3 and Burst 4, be aware that some of the bass drum notes will end in unison with backbeats on the snare drum.

Make sure you develop the ability to play the bass drum and snare together at places that they should match. This will develop your ability to end a double bass drum phrase that might double up with the hands on toms, cymbals, and other sound sources.

Burst 3. Five Notes with the Feet

Burst 4. Nine Notes with the Feet

Rhythmic Interpretation

"BURSTING OUT OF HERE"

This etude demonstrates some possibilities with the bursts in duple feel. Follow the form, and play exactly what is written for the double bass and snare drums. Use your imagination to create parts for hi-hat, ride cymbal, and other sound sources along with the etude.

Henrique De Almeida

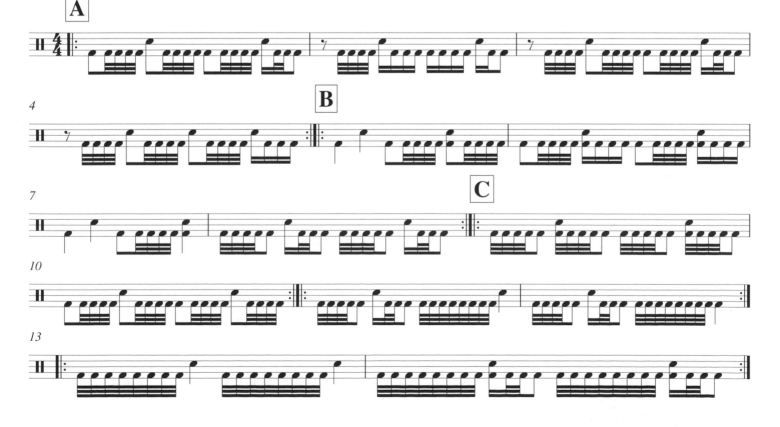

LESSON 7

Triple-Feel Bursts

When playing an eighth-note *triplet* shuffle feel in a pop/rock/Latin groove, a burst usually will be in sextuplets. Instead of three notes per beat, it would be six notes per beat.

When playing burst 3 and burst 4, some of the bass drum notes will end in unison with backbeats on the snare drum.

Make sure you develop the ability to play the bass drum and snare together at places where they should match. This will develop your ability to end a double bass drum phrase in unison with other parts of the kit, such as a crash cymbal. It will also develop your ability to play a constant double bass rhythm while "passing by" accented notes played in unison with the toms, cymbals, and other sound sources.

TYPES OF BURSTS

Triple Bursts
1 & 2 with
Rhythmic
Interpretation
(0:00–0:06)

Burst 1. Three Notes with the Feet, One Note with the Hands

Triple Bursts
1 & 2 with
Rhythmic
Interpretation
(0:06–0:11)

Burst 2. Six Notes with the Feet, One Note with the Hands

Triple Bursts
1 & 2 with
Rhythmic
Interpretation
(0:11–0:23)

Rhythmic Interpretation

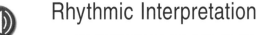

Burst 3. Four Notes with the Feet

Triple Bursts 3 & 4 with Rhythmic Interpretation (0:00–0:05)

Burst 4. Seven Notes with the Feet

Triple Bursts 3 & 4 with Rhythmic Interpretation (0:05–0:11)

Rhythmic Interpretation

Triple Bursts 3 & 4 with Rhythmic Interpretation (0:11–0:22)

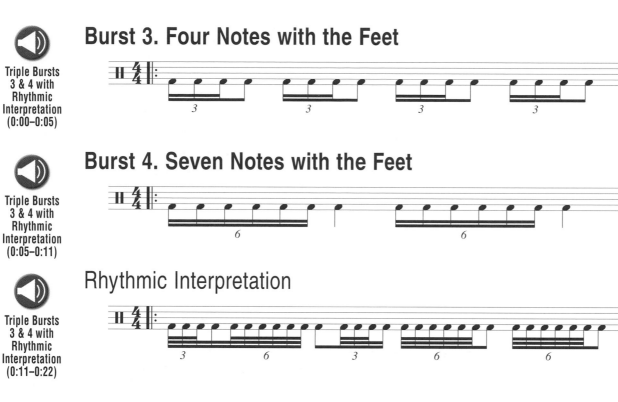

"BURSTING OUT OF THERE"

This etude demonstrates some possibilities with the bursts in triple feel. Follow the form, and play exactly what is written for the double bass and snare drums. Use your imagination to play parts for hi-hat, ride cymbal, and other sound sources along with the etude.

Henrique De Almeida

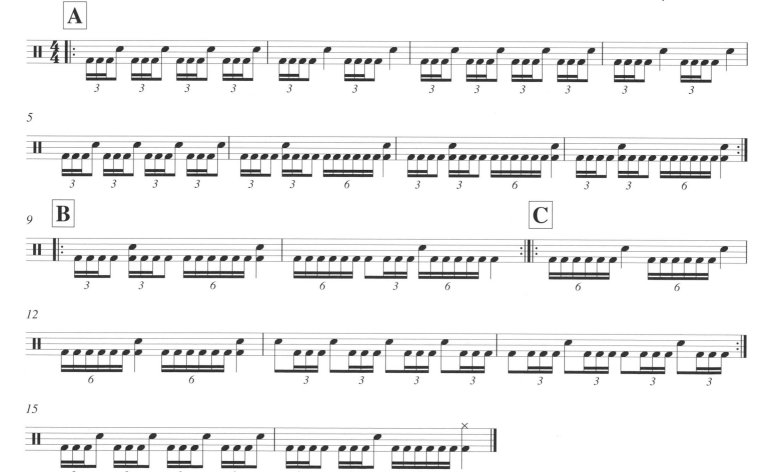

Basic Double Strokes

Play quarter notes or eighth notes on the hi-hat or ride cymbal. Play a simple backbeat on beats 2 and 4 while exercising double-stroke variations with the feet.

EXERCISES

Exercise 1. Right-Foot Lead Doubles

Exercise 2. Right-Foot Lead Reverse Doubles

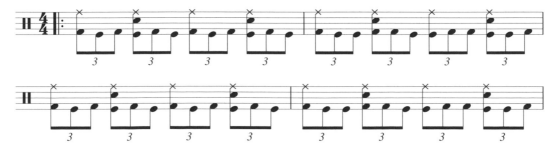

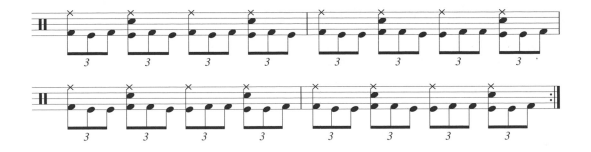

Exercise 3. Left-Foot Lead Doubles

Exercise 4. Left-Foot Lead Reverse Doubles

Exercise 5. Reversing the Singles

Exercise 6. Reversing the Doubles

FILLING IN: LINEAR EXERCISES

Triplet Feel

In this exercise, we are developing the rhythmic interpretation of quarter notes and eighth notes. Play the main melodic ideas with the hands while filling in the spaces with the feet.

Here are five basic ways to play this type of exercise:

1. Play your hand ideas with both hands together, and fill in the spaces with the feet.

2. Play alternating hands: R, L, etc. now using toms, cymbals, etc.

3. Play a cymbal ostinato with the right hand while playing hand ideas with the left hand.

4. Play a cymbal ostinato with the left hand while playing hand ideas with the right hand.

5. Play hand ideas in unison, but place one of the hands on a cymbal while the other hand is playing any drums.

Stickings:

1. Unison: Right and Left

2. RL Alternating

3. Rests are filled with triplets in the double bass until the next snare drum hit.

4. After you get comfortable playing in a solo or fill mode, incorporate hi-hat and ride ostinatos, and practice in a groove type of feel.

**Triplet Feel
Linear Exercises**

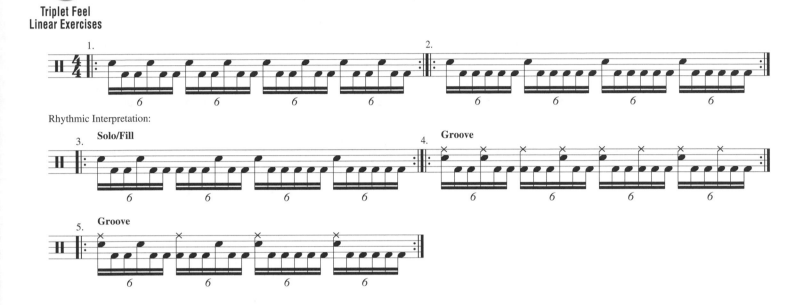

Rhythmic Interpretation:

"LINEAR TRIPLETS" ETUDE

This etude explores many possibilities using the linear approach.

Henrique De Almeida

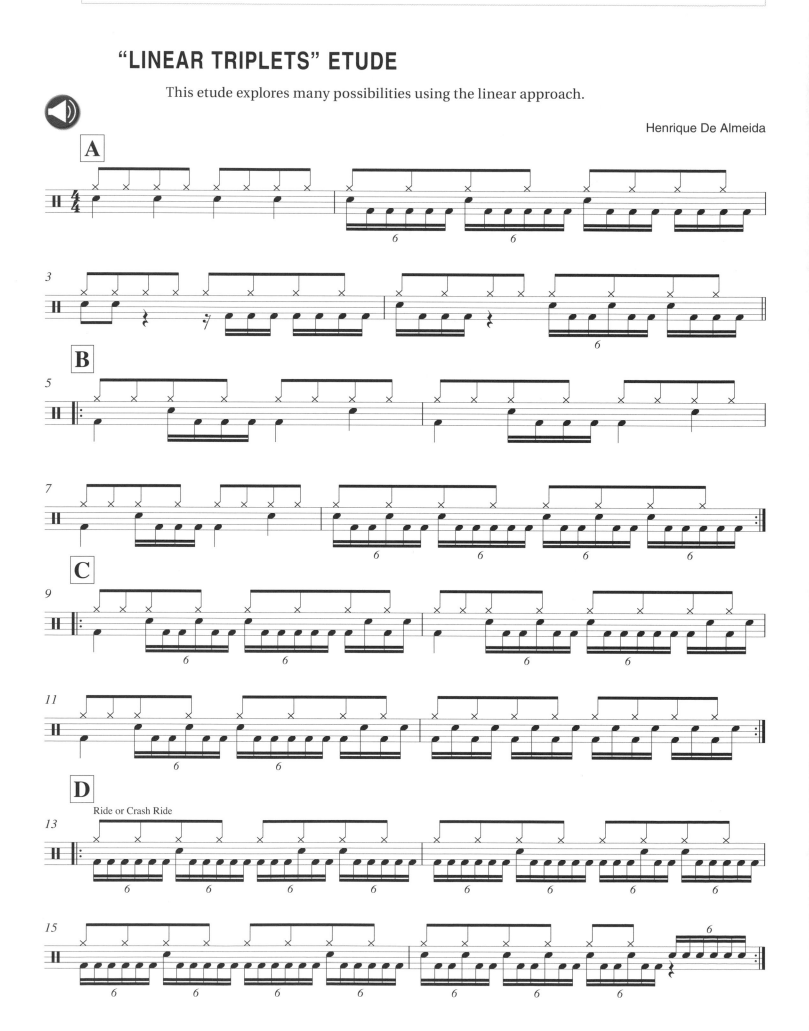

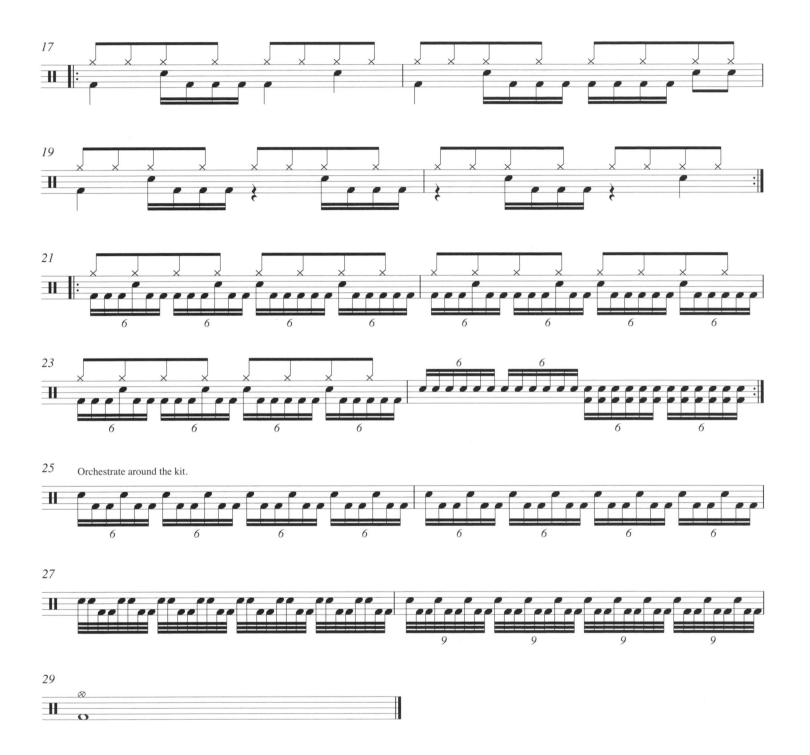

Double Strokes in Duple Feel

Play quarter notes or eighth notes with the hi-hat or ride cymbal. Play a simple backbeat on 2 and 4 while exercising double-stroke variations with the feet.

EXERCISES

Exercise 1. Right-Foot Lead Doubles

Exercise 2. Right-Foot Lead Reverse Doubles

Exercise 3. Left-Foot Lead Doubles

Exercise 4. Left-Foot Lead Reverse Doubles

Exercise 5. Reversing the Singles

Exercise 6. Reversing the Doubles

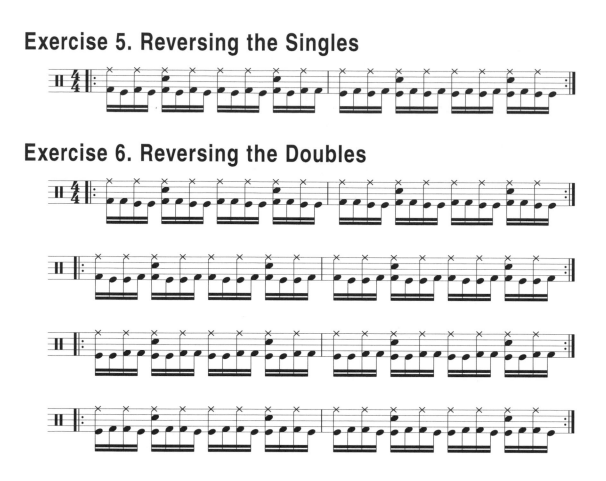

FILLING IN: LINEAR EXERCISES
Duple Feel

Here, we are developing the rhythmic interpretation of quarter notes and eighth notes. Play the main melodic ideas with the hands while filling in the spaces with the feet.

Stickings:

1. Unison: Right and Left

2. Alternating: Right and Left

Rests are filled with triplets double bass until the next snare drum hit.

After you get comfortable playing in a solo or fill mode, incorporate hi-hat and ride ostinatos and practice in a groove type of feel.

Use the same five ways of practicing them as described previously (see page 30/linear).

**Duple Feel
Linear Exercise**

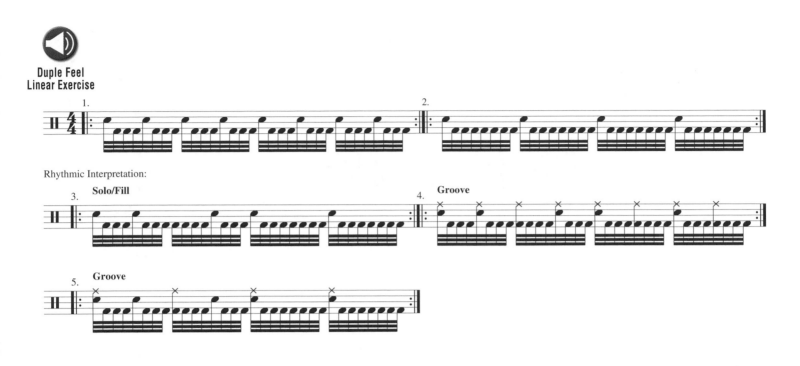

Rhythmic Interpretation:

"LINEAR DUPLE FEEL" ETUDE

This etude explores many possibilities using the linear approach, now in duple feel.

Henrique De Almeida

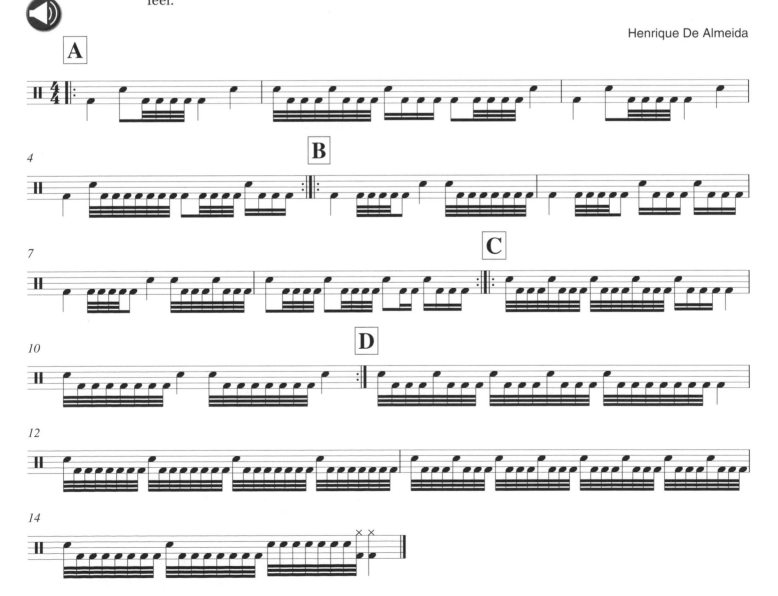

False Triplets

FALSE TRIPLET ROLL

False triplets gives the listener the false impression that the drummer is playing constant triplets with the feet, when in reality, there are notes being inserted with the hands, thus forming a combination of hands/feet figures.

SINGLE-HAND EXERCISES

Exercise 1. RH on Floor Tom

Play eighth notes on the floor tom with the right hand while filling in sextuplets with the double bass. Try to create the illusion that all is being played with the feet. You must try matching the volume and articulation played with your feet. The tuning of your floor tom will also determine how closely its tonality matches your bass drum sound.

False Triplet Roll,
Single-Hand Exercises
(0:00–0:07)

Exercise 2. LH on High Tom

This is the same concept as exercise 1, but with the left hand on the high tom for different color.

False Triplet Roll,
Single-Hand Exercises
(0:09–0:16)

Exercise 3. Reading Eighth Notes

Play eighth notes on the snare drum while inserting sextuplets with the feet in between the snare notes. You can use RL or LR sticking.

Exercise 4. Reading Quarter Notes

Play quarter notes on the snare drum. Play false triplets to complete the rest of the beat cycle. Note that the remaining five notes are played with two double bass hits, one floor tom hit (right hand), and another two double bass hits.

Exercise 5. RH Solo/Fill Ideas

Exercise 6. LH Solo/Fill Ideas

Exercise 7. RH Groove Ideas

Exercise 8. LH Reading Text

This is the same as exercise 7, but with the left hand reading the text. So, the right hand now plays quarter notes on a ride, right hi-hat (if extra hi-hat available), and/or cowbell, etc. The left hand will be moving from the high tom to the snare drum, reading the text with the snare drum, then going back to the high tom filling in all the rests with false triplets between the high tom and double bass.

**False Triplet Roll,
Single-Hand Exercises
(1:01–1:09)**

Exercise 9. LH Reading Text While the RH Moves Back and Forth

This is an example of left hand using false triplets, now incorporating a cowbell and hi-hat sound.

**False Triplet Roll,
Single-Hand Exercises
(1:10–1:17)**

Once you understand the false triplet concept, practice them any way you want. Here it is a basic starting point for false triplet explorations.

1. R DB DB (RH and two double bass hits)

2. L DB DB (LH and two double bass hits)

3. R DB DB with LH playing an ostinato

4. L DB DB with RH playing an ostinato

5. R DB DB L DB DB (alternating RH lead)

6. L DB DB R DB DB (alternating LH lead)

7. U DB DB (unison: both RH and LH plays at the same time)

8. Play through the *Stick Control* book (by L. Stone) with false triplets.

9. Read text mixing all the above to create improvisation of orchestration.

10. Freely improvise solo, fill, and groove ideas within a music context.

11. Chose a meter, style, and groove. Then insert false triplets.

FALSE TRIPLETS TIMETABLE

This exercise will help you gain speed and rhythmic flexibility using false triplets. Practice each figure until you are comfortable with the rhythms. Then, move to the next one, and so forth. Eventually, you will be able to play from the beginning to the end without stopping. Then, go from the end to the beginning, without stopping. This will create a rolling effect, from slow to fast to slow. Use a metronome with this exercise so you hear the tempo at all times. Note that some bars break across systems to end.

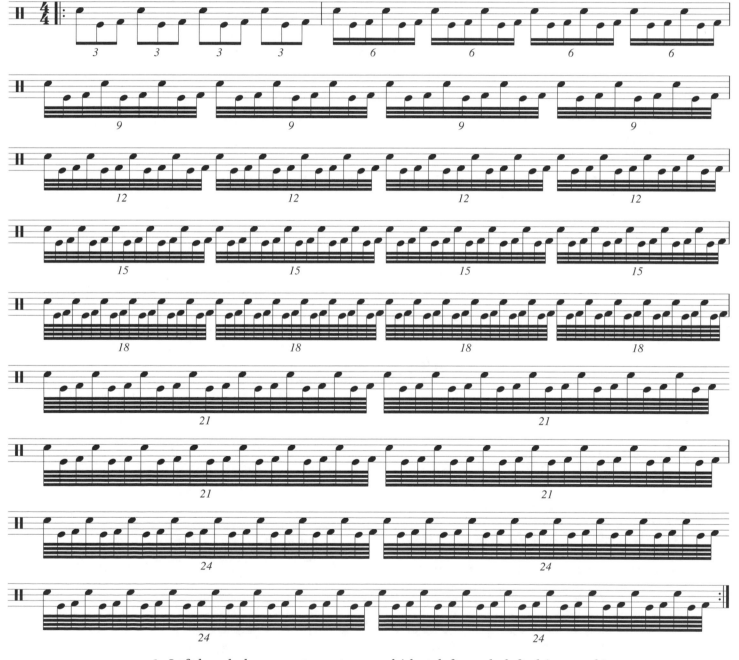

1. Left hand plays quarter notes on a hi-hat, left crash, left china, and/or cowbell.

2. Right hand plays a flow of false triplets between floor tom and double bass.

3. Right hand moves from the floor tom to the snare drum and plays text on the snare drum, returning to the floor filling up all the rests with false triplets.

"THE B LINE"

This etude explores some unusual rhythms. It is inspired by one of my teachers, Mr. Gary Chafee, and one of my all-times heroes, Mr. Steve Gadd.

Sections A to C

- Start with a forte accent on the bass drum and crash. Stay strong until B.

- At B, I usually think of Steve Gadd and a bit of the great drummer and Berklee grad, Steve Smith. Contrast the triplets and the sixteenth- and thirty-second-note figures. Incorporate the indicated dynamics.

- At the third bar of B, we have the false-triples application, as well as at measure 13, before going back to the top.

- Section C continues with mixed rhythms containing groups of five and six notes, and bursts of four and five notes.

Sections D and E

- Snare drum notes around the backbeat here could be played as ghosted notes.

- Note the quintuplets and septuplets.

- Then we recapitulate the A theme going to a coda-like section.

- Getting softer and softer. Think Anthony Cirone, here! Then BANG! A power fill on the end.

This is a bit challenging but very fun solo to play. Have fun!

The B Line

Henrique De Almeida

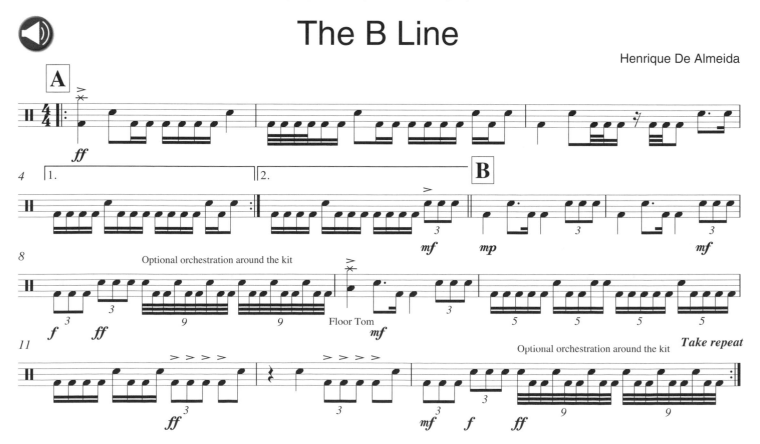

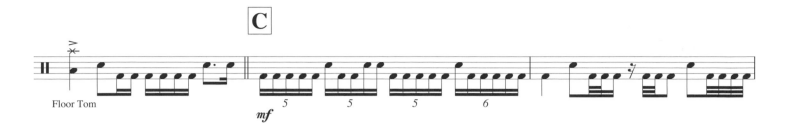

Get softer and softer each time to a *pp*. *Play 4 times*

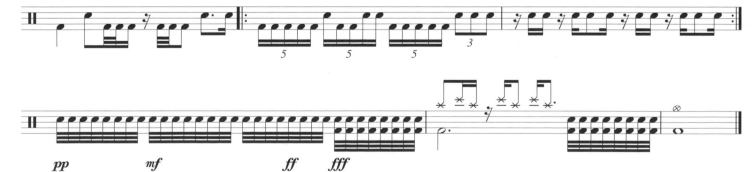

Floor Tom

Quads

SINGLE QUADS

Here, we utilize the four limbs to create a fast roll. This technique can be very colorful, because each limb could play a different sound source. It basically consists of hand-foot-hand-foot, etc.

Explore the following sticking:

1. RLRL

2. LRLR

3. Adding accents to the hands such as on every 3, 4, 5, 6, 7, 8, etc.

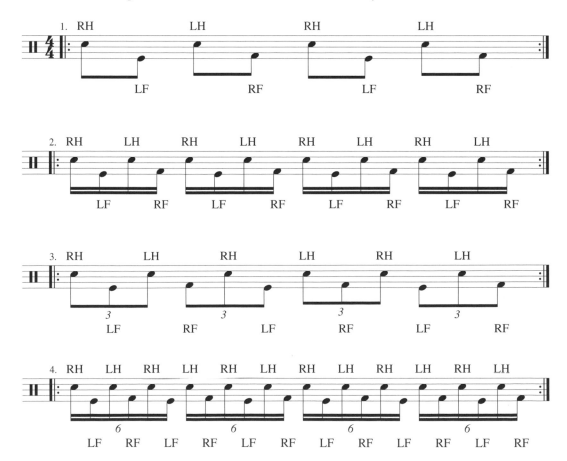

Single Quads Timetable

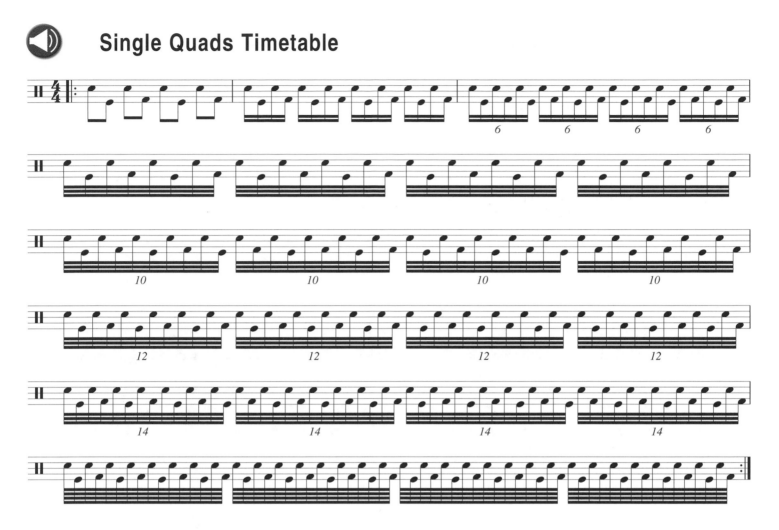

Quasi-Quads

This will sound similar to "Single Quads." It is now played with one hand. This leaves the other hand free to play either ostinatos and/or grooves, or to improvise solos and fills.

The sticking can be:

1. RRRR…

2. LLLL…

3. Play the "Single Quads" timetable above in lesson 10, but now with the quasi-quads.

Quasi Quads
(0:00–0:10)

1. Play Quasi-Quads.

R   R   R   R   *etc.*   *Also try: L L L L etc.*

Quasi Quads
(0:10–0:32)

2. Add left-hand ideas on top.

NOTE: Use this concept to develop ideas for grooves, fills, and soloing applications. For flexibility, try reading rhythms text such as the Ted Reed book and others' books.

DOUBLE QUADS TIMETABLE

Double quads are played two notes with the hands and two notes with the feet.

Suggested Sticking:

1. RH lead singles

2. LH lead singles

3. RH lead doubles

4. LH lead doubles

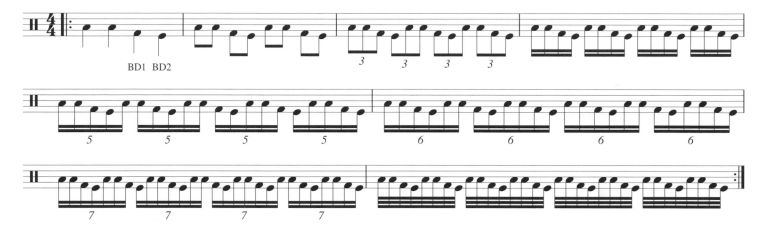

REVERSE DOUBLE QUADS TIMETABLE

This is the same as "Double Quads Timetable," but now starting with the double bass.

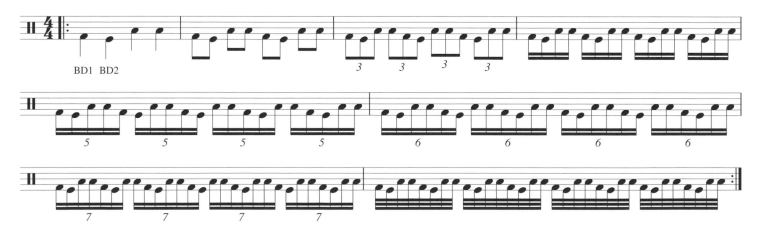

"HEAVY WEATHER" (A.K.A. ROLLING BLAST)

This etude explores many concepts presented in previous lessons, including quasi-quads on the intro, linear triplets at C, and false triplets at D, among other techniques.

Heavy Weather

AKA "Rolling Blast" on YouTube

Henrique De Almeida

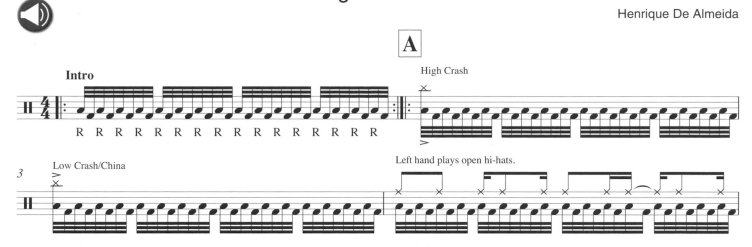

D

14
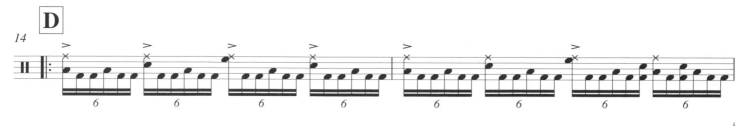

16
To Coda ⊕

A'

18 Add backbeat

20
D.S. al Coda

⊕ Coda

22

24

26

"SIX REASONS"

This etude explores many different concepts presented in previous lessons, including triplet-feel grooves from the endurance exercises, linear triplets, quads, double quads, false triplets, and more.

Six Reasons

Henrique De Almeida

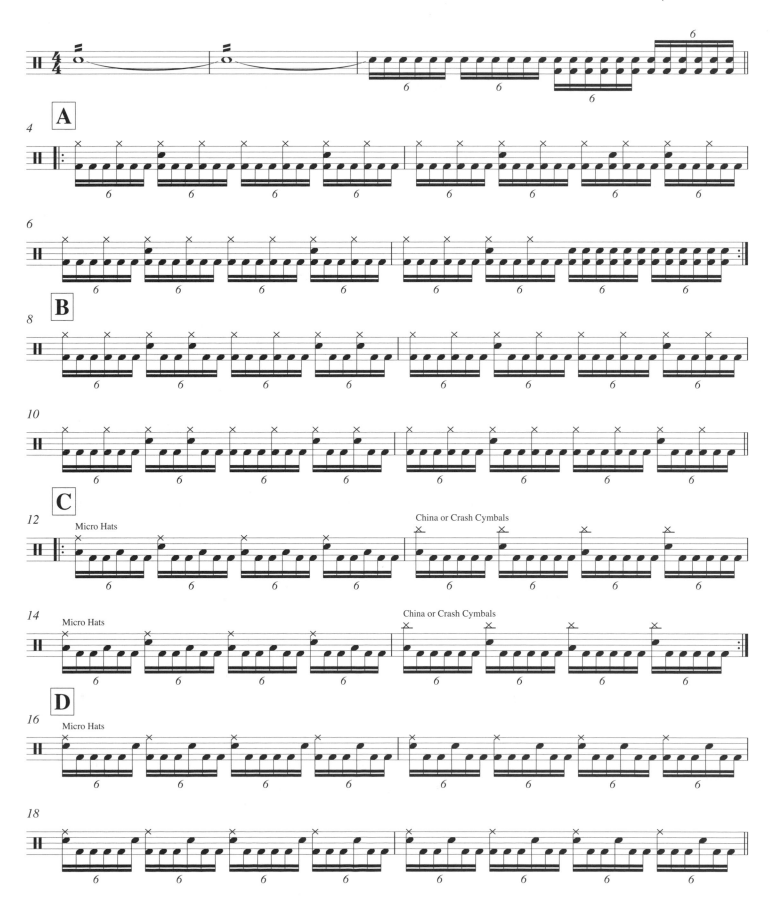

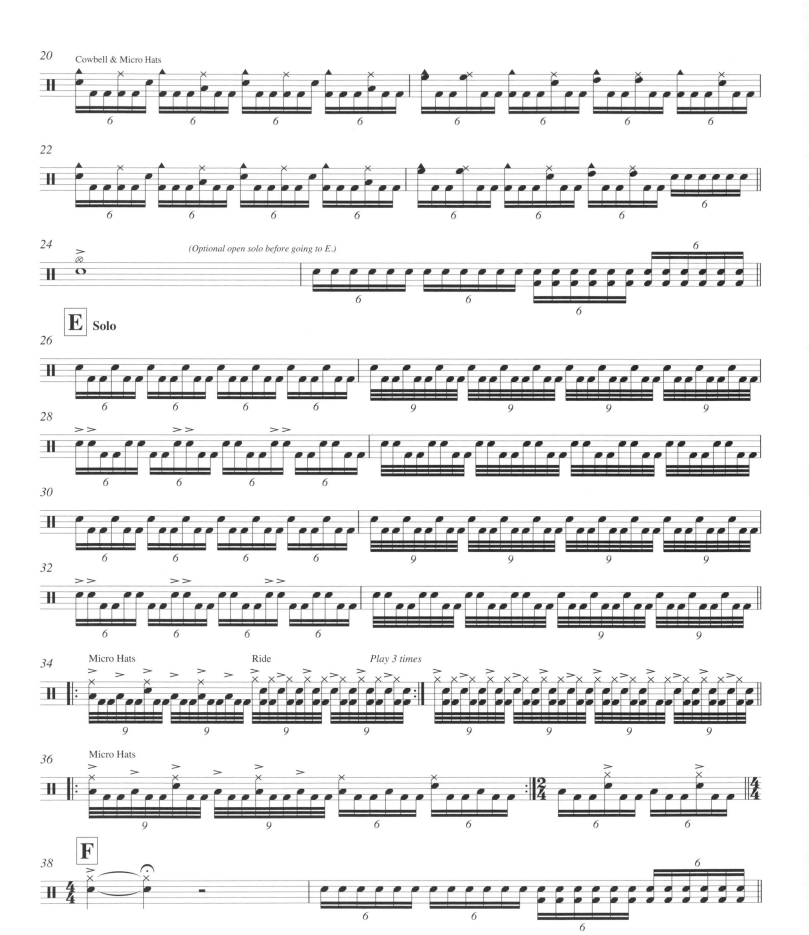

⊕ Coda

LESSON 12

Power Fills

TWO- AND FIVE-NOTE FILLS WITH THE HANDS

We can play eighth notes by using exercise 1, and quarter notes by playing either exercise 2 or exercise 3.

Note that the accented notes in exercises 4 and 5 are representing eighth- and quarter-note figures that are being embellished with the power fills. With this concept, you can then systematically read text such as the Ted Reed *Syncopation* book and others. You can interpret drum charts as well—any music that you are playing that calls for such a texture.

Exercise 1. Two-Note Groupings

Play two notes with the hands, followed by two notes with the feet.

Exercise 2. Five-Note Groupings

Play five notes with the hands, followed by two notes with the feet.

Exercise 3. Six-Note Groupings

Play six notes with the hands, followed by two notes with the feet.

Exercise 4. Interpreting Eighth and Quarter Notes

Exercise 5. Power Fill Ideas

LINEAR FILLS

Fills with Unison Bass Drum and Cymbals

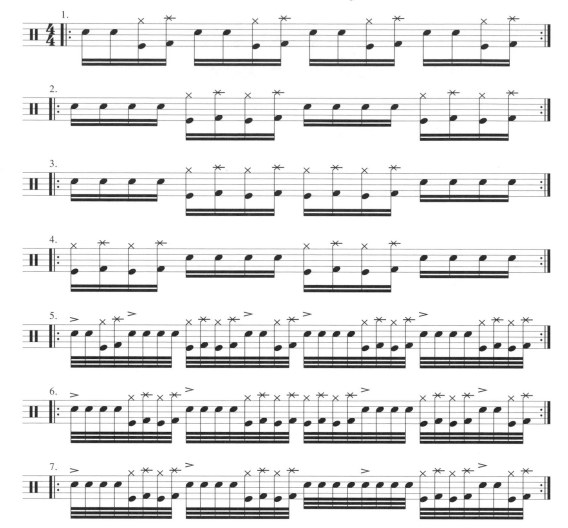

REVERSE LINEAR POWER FILLS

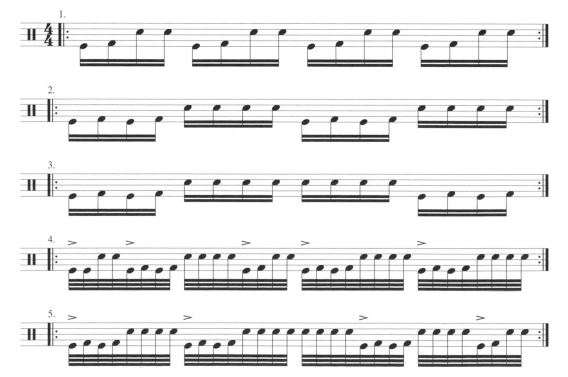

REVERSE LINEAR FILLS WITH UNISON BASS DRUM AND CYMBALS

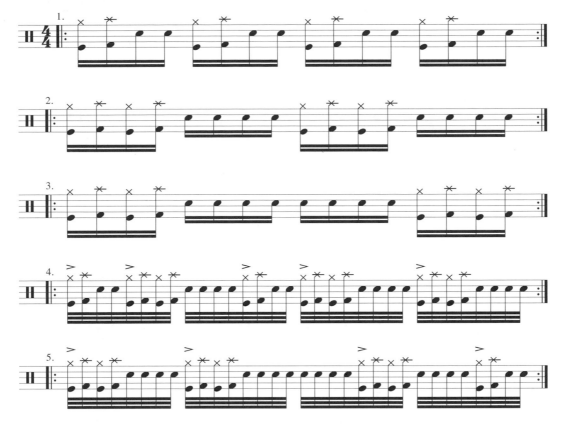

TRIPLET FEEL

Linear Fills with Triplet Feel

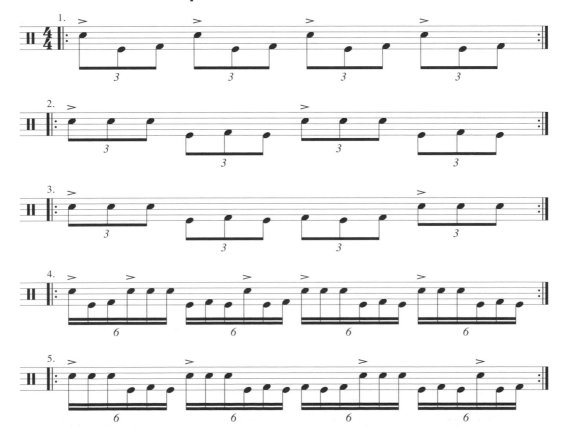

Linear Fills with Unison Bass Drum and Cymbals

Reverse Linear Power Fills

Reverse Fills with Unison Bass Drum and Cymbals

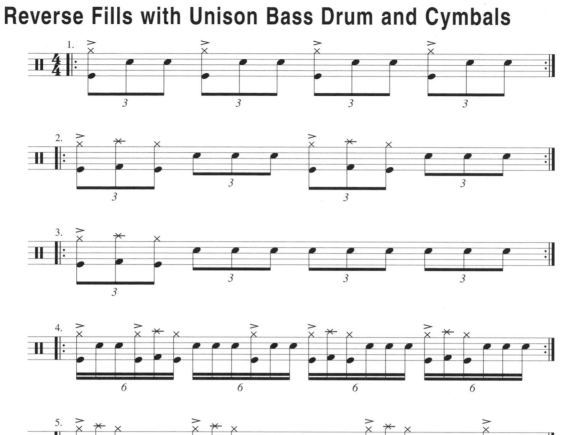

"PARADOUBLES"

This etude explores unisons and polyrhythmic possibilities, as well as other techniques.

Henrique De Almeida

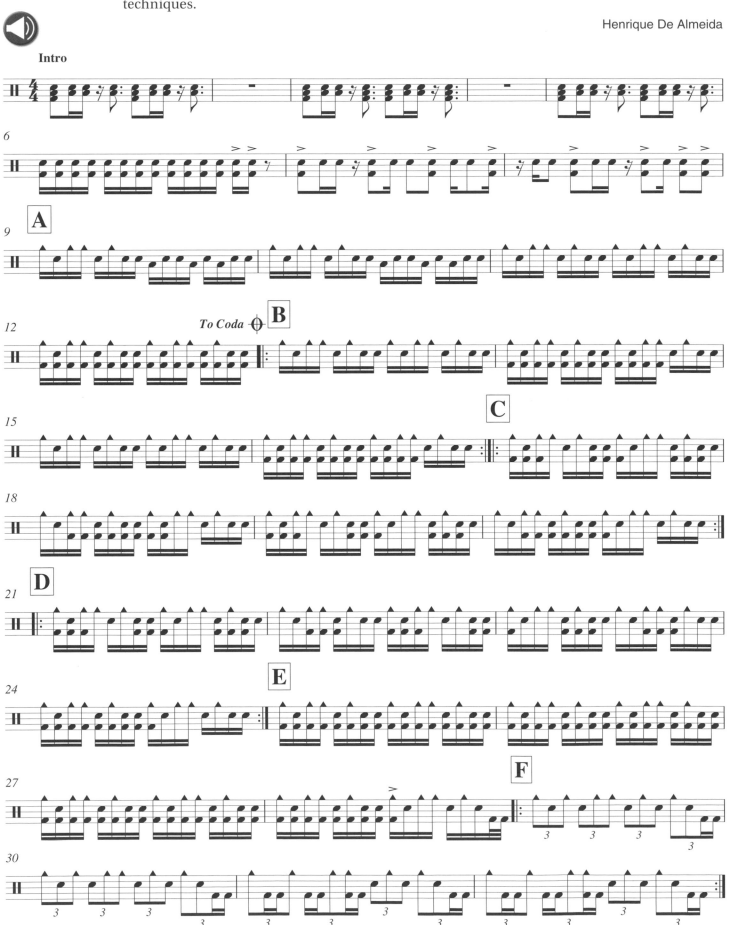

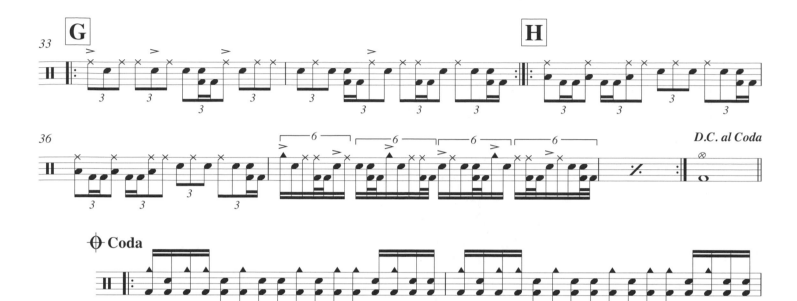

ABOUT THE AUTHOR

Photo by Jonathan Betz

Henrique De Almeida has recorded and toured nationally and internationally with the USAFA premier jazz big band the Falconaires and the USAFA rock band Blue Steel. He performed for two presidents of the United States, a vice president, and a secretary of defense. He performed several times at Carnegie Hall. Henrique has worked, recorded, and/or tour with a large musical range of artists: Gloria Estefan, Nat Adderley, Bill Cosby, Antonio Hart, Christopher Holiday, Donny McCaslin, Chris Speed, Igor Butman, Dave Valentin, Scotty Barnhart, Tiger Okoshi, Larry Coryell, Jeff Berlin, Stanton Moore, Billy Cobham, Nelson Rangel, Jeff Narell, Ira Sullivan, Victor Mendoza, Jerry Bergonzi, Danilo Perez, Phil Wilson, Dave Samuels, Baron Brown, Matt Garrison, Bill Summers, Hilton Ruiz, Betty Carter, Willie Williams, Nando Lauria (from the Pat Metheny Group), and Brazilian pop stars: Alceu Valença, Gilberto Gill, Raul De Souza, Luiz Gonzaga, Hermeto Pascoal, Brian Lynch, Ronnie Matthews, David Williams, Luciana Souza, Katy Webster, and Oskar Cartaya, among others.

Henrique leads his own groups, the Brazilian Jazz Project and the jazz/rock fusion group World News. He is a clinician for Yamaha Drums, LP (Latin Percussion), Vic Firth sticks, Paiste cymbals, HQ pads, Evans drumheads, and Earthworks microphones. A published author and producer/composer, he has educational materials available from Carl Fischer Music and Berklee Press.

As a composer, he created original music used in television advertising campaigns for companies such as HBO, Victoria's Secret, and Australian David Jones Department stores. He writes articles for *Modern Drummer* magazine, and has performed at PASIC convention and numerous jazz festivals around the world.

Henrique is associate professor at Berklee College of Music. He is a Berklee graduate in jazz composition, and he holds a masters degree in music performance from the University of Southern Mississippi.

For more information, music, books, and DVDs by Henrique De Almeida, visit henriquedealmeida.com.